IF F(TO:

Greater Than a Tourist Book Series
Reviews from Readers

I think the series is wonderful and beneficial for tourists to get information before visiting the city.

-Seckin Zumbul, Izmir Turkey

I am a world traveler who has read many trip guides but this one really made a difference for me. I would call it a heartfelt creation of a local guide expert instead of just a guide.

-Susy, Isla Holbox, Mexico

New to the area like me, this is a must have!

 -Joe, Bloomington, USA

This is a good series that gets down to it when looking for things to do at your destination without having to read a novel for just a few ideas.

-Rachel, Monterey, USA

Good information to have to plan my trip to this destination.

-Pennie Farrell, Mexico

Great ideas for a port day.

-Mary Martin USA

Aptly titled, you won't just be a tourist after reading this book. You'll be greater than a tourist!

-Alan Warner, Grand Rapids, USA

Even though I only have three days to spend in San Miguel in an upcoming visit, I will use the author's suggestions to guide some of my time there. An easy read - with chapters named to guide me in directions I want to go.

-Robert Catapano, USA

Great insights from a local perspective! Useful information and a very good value!

-Sarah, USA

This series provides an in-depth experience through the eyes of a local. Reading these series will help you to travel the city in with confidence and it'll make your journey a unique one.

-Andrew Teoh, Ipoh, Malaysia

GREATER THAN A TOURIST- OPORTO PORTUGAL

50 Travel Tips from a Local

Mariana Lambertini

Cover designed by: Ivana Stamenkovic
Cover Image: https://pixabay.com/en/boat-ancient-barrel-oporto-521351/

Edited by:

CZYK Publishing Since 2011.

Greater Than a Tourist
Visit our website at www.GreaterThanaTourist.com

Lock Haven, PA
ISBN: 9781790913916

>TOURIST

50 TRAVEL TIPS FROM A LOCAL

BOOK DESCRIPTION

Are you excited about planning your next trip?

Do you want to try something new?

Would you like some guidance from a local?

If you answered yes to any of these questions, then this Greater Than a Tourist book is for you.

Greater Than a Tourist- Oporto by Mariana Lambertini offers the inside scoop on Oporto. Most travel books tell you how to travel like a tourist. Although there is nothing wrong with that, as part of the Greater Than a Tourist series, this book will give you travel tips from someone who has lived at your next travel destination.

In these pages, you will discover advice that will help you throughout your stay. This book will not tell you exact addresses or store hours but instead will give you excitement and knowledge from a local that you may not find in other smaller print travel books.

Travel like a local. Slow down, stay in one place, and get to know the people and the culture. By the time you finish this book, you will be eager and prepared to travel to your next destination.

TABLE OF CONTENTS

12. Boavista (Palácio de Cristal, Casa da Música and Serralves Museum and Parka and a bit far, Parque da Cidade)
13. Seaside (Foz e Matosinhos)
14. Riverside (Bairro Sé, Ribeira and the city Vila Nova de Gaia to the wine)
15. Music and Festivals
16. Culture (Bombarda, Serralves..)
17. "Miradouros"
18. Food
19. Wine
20. Beer
21. Coffees – Traditional ones to the Trendiest
22. Weather
23. Work in Oporto
24. Airport
25. Hostels – The best ones to stay
26. Hotels – The best ones to stay
27. Transports
28. Parties You Don't Want to Miss
29. Markets
30. Expositions
31. Churches and Cemeteries
32. Erasmus Program
33. Vila Nova de Gaia
34. River

DEDICATION

This book is dedicated to Oporto citizens that will welcome you, make you feel at home and thinking about another time to return to the city.

ABOUT THE AUTHOR

Mariana Lambertini is a communication professional that has born in Oporto and lived there until her 26 years. Since she has studied there and did her the university and grew there it is difficult to find something in Oporto that she can not be aware of.

Nowadays she works as content creator and has studying storytelling in order to become more and more specialized on telling and write the greatest stories, fictional or non-fictional.

During her life has lived in Oporto, Lisbon and also in Bogota and already traveled to a lot of countries so you might will find another travel guides that she had written.

HOW TO USE THIS BOOK

The Greater Than a Tourist book series was written by someone who has lived in an area for over three months. The goal of this book is to help travelers either dream or experience different locations by providing opinions from a local. The author has made suggestions based on their own experiences. Please do your own research before traveling to the area in case the suggested places are unavailable.

Travel Advisories: As a first step in planning any trip abroad, check the Travel Advisories for your intended destination.
https://travel.state.gov/content/travel/en/traveladvisories/traveladvisories.html

FROM THE PUBLISHER

Traveling can be one of the most important parts of a person's life. The anticipation and memories that you have are some of the best. As a publisher of the Greater Than a Tourist book series, as well as the popular 50 Things to Know book series, we strive to help you learn about new places, spark your imagination, and inspire you. Wherever you are and whatever you do I wish you safe, fun, and inspiring travel.

Lisa Rusczyk Ed. D.
CZYK Publishing

OUR STORY

Traveling is a passion of the "Greater than a Tourist" series creator. Lisa studied abroad in college, and for their honeymoon Lisa and her husband toured Europe. During her travels to Malta, an older man tried to give her some advice based on his own experience living on the island since he was a young boy. She was not sure if she should talk to the stranger but was interested in his advice. When traveling to some places she was wary to talk to locals because she was afraid that they weren't being genuine. Through her travels, Lisa learned how much locals had to share with tourists. Lisa created the "Greater Than a Tourist" book series to help connect people with locals. A topic that locals are very passionate about sharing.

WELCOME TO
> TOURIST

INTRODUCTION

I haven't been everywhere but it's on my list.

Susan Sontag,
writer

Porto, situated in the north of Portugal, is the second most important city in the country, after the capital Lisbon.

Around 200 hundred thousand people live in the city and it has been changing a lot because the tourism has grown in an exponential way and nowadays is one of the trendiest places to travel in Europe.

In fact, Porto won the European Best Destination title in 2012, 2014 and 2017. And this conquer spotlighted the city that wasn't really known a few decades ago.

Porto is a small city, compared to other cities in Europe, so is the ideal place to a weekend trip because is not an huge city so you can enjoy it in three, four days. But if you manage to pass a few days more in the city you will enjoy it completely and in every term of its culture and way of living. Also you can go to other cities near or even you can make a full trip around Portugal, that would be perfect and in fact it is the best choice.

Before we start to talk about the places to visit and the things to know, let's just make a little resume about the history of the city. If you have interest about this area and you always wanna know all the depep historical facts about the cities you travel to, I advise you to search more about this facts because, as any other european city, Porto has an important history background.

It originates in a Celtic , pre-Roman settlement . In Roman time it was designated Cale or Portus Cale , being the origin of the name of Portugal.

On 27 April 711 AD the Muslim invasion of the Iberian Peninsula began, with the landing in Gibraltar of a Moorish army of 9000 men, led by Táriq Ibn Ziyad . In 714 take Lisbon, and 715 Islamic forces reach the northern part of what we now know as Portugal, taking the main towns and cities such as Porto and Braga . In 716 have almost the entire Peninsula was under the control of the Umayyad Caliphate , with the exception of a small mountainous area of Asturias, where Christian resistance took refuge.

After a century and a half, in 868, the first attempts of definitive reconquest appear, Vímara Peres , founder of the land of Portugal, made an important contribution in the conquest of the territory, thus restoring the city of Portucale .

Porto Cathedral with the Old House of the House in the background. Finally, after two centuries after the start of the invasion, in 999 a noble and valiant noblemen Gascon among whom was D. Nónego bishop of Vendôme in France and later bishop of Porto went with a big mouth of the Armada River Douro, to expel the Moors. This armada, which became known as the Armada dos Gascões associated with D. Munio Viegas "plucked" the city from Porto to the Moors to dedicate it to the Virgin Mother of God. After this battle, D. Munio and the "French" tried to rebuild the Port. They erected the old and strong walls, and in the highest part of the city they founded a well-strengthened and carved fortress which, after Count Henry, served as a habitation for the bishops to whom it was donated. The tower and the main door were the work of D. Néongo, who, in memory of the mother country, named it Vandoma's door , and on the tower's front he erected the sanctuary, where he placed the image of Our Lady of Porto , which he had already brought with you from France. In 1111, Therese of Leo , mother of the future first king of Portugal, granted the bishop D. Hugo the couto of Porto. The image of Our Lady is part of the city's weapons. Hence the fact that Porto is also known as "the city of the Virgin", epithets to which must be added those of " Old, Very Noble, Always Loyal and Invicta, " which have been attributed to it over the centuries and following valiant of its inhabitants, and that they were ratified by decree of D. Maria II of Portugal .

It was within its walls that the marriage of King João I was effected with the English princess D. Filipa de Lencastre . The city was the birthplace of Prince Henry , known as the Infant of Sagres or The Navigator.

Due to the sacrifices that the city made to support the preparation of the navy that left in 1415 for the conquest of Ceuta , the population of the Port offered to the expeditionaries all the available meat, being only with the "guts" to feed the natural of Porto won the nickname "tripeiros", an expression more tender than pejorative. This is also the reason why the traditional dish of the city is still, today, the " Tripas à moda do Porto ". There is a confraternity specially dedicated to this typical dish.

In the Eighteenth and nineteenth centuries, the city played a key role in defending the ideals of liberalism more concretely in the battles of the nineteenth century . In fact, the courage with which it supported the siege of the miguelista troops during the civil war of 1832-34 and the valorous deeds undertaken by its inhabitants - the famous Siege of Porto - were worth even the attribution, by the queen D. Maria II, of the a title - unique among the other cities of Portugal - of Invicta Cidade do Porto (still present today in the list of its arms), whence the epithet with which it is frequently mentioned by antonomasia - the « Invicta ». It houses one of its many churches -Lapa - the heart of D. Pedro IV of Portugal , who offered it to the population of the city in honor of the contribution given by its inhabitants to the liberal cause.

City graced with the Military Order of the Tower and Sword of Valor, Loyalty and Merit on April 26, 1919.

1. TOURISM

On the last few years Portugal and specially Porto is been a desire destiny for a lot of tourists around Europe (mainly). But from another continents as well.

These changes made so much difference in the city and in the remodeling of the city center that we normally call that the Ryanair Effect. When Ryanair inaugurated a base in Porto, a lot of people start to come to the city and enjoyed it so much that it becomes a desire destination, and it wasn't at all until there.

The flux of people made the city get more modern, walkable, european and a desired place to go. The spot of Portugal is not only Lisbon, the sun light city, it is also the grey, melancholic but really happy at the same time, city of Porto.

During the year a lot of people come to visit the city and other cities near (like Braga and Guimarães). And that's why this guide is more useful now than any time before.

You can discover the city by a person that was born there. Now everything about the day and night life, the most beautiful neighborhoods and sightseeings. Aldo you can discover some interesting facts about the students, the businesses, the foreigners living there and the tourists.

Porto will always have a debt with the tourists, but a good one, not in bad terms. What made the city get better during the last years were in major part the tourists and obviously the development of the city by itself.

2. CITY AREAS

Architecture is also an important point in Porto, is even one of the most recognized places to study Architecture in the world, our public University made as well a possibility for us to grow a lot and have a lot of investment in this area. If you have interest in this area or if you are an architect you already heard about Alvaro Siza Vieira (Pritzker em 1992 e Wolf em 2001) e Eduardo Souto de Moura (Pritzker em 2011 e Wolf em 2013).

Stepping this importance of the architecture, let's talk about the city areas by itself.

First, this is harder to explain in a few words. Mainly, we can "divide" the city in areas to visit like: the "center" – not geographically but the way the city is divided to visit and how we use to recognize (Aliados, Clérigos, Cordoaria, Cedofeita); the shopping area (Santa Catarina and Mercado do Bolhão); Boavista (Palácio de Cristal, Casa da Música and Serralves Museum and Park and a bit far, Parque da Cidade); Seaside (Foz and Matosinhos); Riverside (Sé, Ribeira and the city Vila Nova de Gaia to the wine). Then we can appreciate that these areas are really different one from another which makes the city a versatile one, with riverside, seaside, typical neighborhoods and fervillant and modern cultural spots.

I will talk about these areas separately now.

3. CITY CENTER

When I say city center it is not a geographic setting but it is a way to describe these areas to the locals and also to better localize them, putting together.

In fact the city center is a large area that corresponds to the shopping area, the city hall area and the night spots and cultural spots as well. These areas are the areas that most changed over the past few years, what we used to call Ryannair Effect, as I told you before.

Inside of city center I need to destak these ones: Aliados, Clérigos, Cordoaria and Cedofeita. Will talk about them separately.

The movement of the city is in fact centred here, that's why we call it city center. The heart of the city could be the description as well.

This is also the area that changed the most over the past few decades. Now we have coffees that are really trend spots, nice hotels that can albergue you and that show how fancy Porto can be. Every time there's an event important on the city, will happen first here. Historically is also an important area.

Let's separate the center and figure out where you need to go if you want history, europe fervillant culture, nightlife or only do some shopping to offer the greatest souvenirs when you get back to your hometown.

4. ALIADOS

Aliados is a great and large avenue where you can see the city hall and imposing buildings. Is situated on the lower part of the city. If you already check for our tomography, you checked that Porto is building from up to down, from typical neighborhoods where most part of people live (like Marquês) until the riverside, the most tourist one. Aliados is in the middle of it.

Here you can check another typical Porto architecture sinal: all the buildings are in granite. In fact, the real avenue that starts on the city hall was until 2006 a green landscape and nowadays is paved by granite as well, with an artificial small lake in the middle and a lot of banks, in granite as well, and only a few trees. This was a polemic transformation at the time, a lot of people were against this "grey transformation" but nowadays everyone is used to it and we can say that was a victorious remodeling. These transformation was made by the architects that I already told you about: Siza Vieira and Souto Moura. Which can prove the importance of them in the city itself.

In the middle of the avenue you can find two statues that represents (and in fact are called by)

Youth and The Boys. They were made by Henrique Moreira, a portuguese sculpture that studied in Porto University - Formed by the Portuguese Academy of Fine Arts, an important Faculty in the University as well. Porto was always an important place for artists as you can see.

On the end of the avenue you can also go to McDonald's but in these case not because you are a tourist that wants to eat something but because this was considered "the most beautiful in the world". Now is a fast food spot but maintains the structure and everything intacted from the time that was the Imperial Cafe, one of the most important in the city. And cafes were also a really important thing on the city and unfortunately nowadays they are all getting modifications, but at least this one remains a little bit the same, although is a sinal of time changing and globalization.

During important dates and events, this avenue receives the people. Every time that F.C.Porto wins an important annual competition, football club fans go there to celebrate. On NYE there's a stage with concerts and there's always fireworks to celebrate another year coming. Also, on the most important night for the city (São João – you will hear about that) there's always concerts and people celebrating here.

Is the municipal center and also a place where the people join to celebrate something.

5. CITY HALL

Right in the middle of the avenue, you can find the city hall building. Is an imposing one with a big importance on the city architecture and formation.

You can visit or you can only see it from the outside and take good photos of it.

6. SÃO BENTO

This train station was designed by the Portuguese architect José Marques da Silva . The construction started in 1896 and was only officially opened on 5 October 1916.

Probably you already saw pictures of our most beautiful train station: São Bento. São Bento is a 20th century railway station and is worldwide known for his historic tiles, on the main lobby, that describe important historical scenes set in the north of the country. There are approximately 20.000 tiles made by Jorge Colaço, an important "azulejador" in our country (and you might know as well that tiles are very important in our country and specially in the North). They are made in a typical New Art style, using light blue colors mostly. They represent events like the battle of valdevez(panel Arcos de Arcos Battle), the presentation of Egas Moniz with his sons to King Afonso VII of Leon and Castile in the 12th Century, the entrance of D. João I and D. Filipa de Lencastre in Porto (entrance panel of John I in Porto) in 1387, the Conquest of Ceuta , in 1415 and so on.

These tiles and lobby are what makes this station one of the most beautiful in the world.

The train station itself receives Nowadays the urban trains that make a lot of journeys everyday to cities really near Porto or even on the surroundings of the city but has a lot of people passing everyday. The large distance train trips are made from Campanhã, the other train station. If you want to go to Lisbon per example, you need to go there and not to São Bento.

7. CLÉRIGOS

You might also have seen pictures of Porto, or maybe you went there before, and you are already familiar with the Tower that you can see in most part of postcards and from some places in the city. Architect Nicolau Nasoni built Clérigos tower on the eighteenth century.

Near the tower you can also visit an excellent and new architecture constructor from where you have a great view and you can take the greatest pictures to the tower to have a bust on your Instagram account. Go to place called Praça de Lisboa on the ground you have expensive fashion stores and also an expensive restaurant and coffee, on the second stage (if we can say that) you have a garden where you can chill and just look to the tower and take your best shot. Also you have a bar that has great parties not only late night but mainly at sunset hour especially on summer.

Obviously, you need to go to Livraria Lello – the most beautiful bookshop in the world and it is another place where supposedly J K Rowling started to imagine the stairs on Hogwarts during the time she lived in the city, teaching English.

8. CORDOARIA E CEDOFEITA

In these areas just go and walk, enter on the stores that are beautiful and modern ones and also the typical ones. If you pass by on Saturdays usually there's street markets that are always good opportunities o buy that souvenir that you cannot forget. Talking about places, go to Centro Português de Fotografia (Portuguese Photography Center) because sometimes there's really good expositions there and also is a beautiful building that was once a prison (a lot of years ago) and also you can check a Camilo Castelo Branco's Statue talking about love and about his novels especially the one call "Amor de Perdição" that he written integrally on the prison (nowadays the Portuguese Photography Center).

Really near there you need to go to Virtudes. A garden where people just stay enjoying the view and drinking beer, but I will explain more about these place when I talk about sightseeing.

9. BOAVISTA

Boavista is a generic name of a part of the western city and it is a center for companies, banks and so it is based on work routines.

The spotlights will have special reference on another topics and they are: Palácio de Cristal, Casa da Música, Mercado da Boavista, Serralves Museum and Park and Parque da Cidade.

10. CASA DA MÚSICA

Let's talk about the main concert hall located on Avenida da Boavista and in fact the most important in the city.

Casa da Música (translating, House of Music) is a recent building, was designed by the Dutch architect Rem Koolhaas as part of the European Capital of Culture event in 2001 (Porto 2001), however, the construction was only completed in 2005 , immediately becoming an icon of the city.

It was planned, as the name indicates, for music and for concerts. The first opening day concert took place with the Clans and Lou Reed,

Inside, the most important element is the main auditorium: Sala Suggia. Has an initial capacity of 1,238 seats, but may vary according to the occasion.

Nowadays it receives a lot of world known musicians and also the most famous orchestra concerts. You can check online if there will be some good concert on the days that you plan to be on the city or you can also go on a tour to know the House and have a good explanation about his construction and effects on the city.

11. PALACIO DE CRISTAL

The most famous garden in the city is "Palacio de Cristal Gardens". This Romantic Gardens are great views to the river and you can stay there almost one day, just walking. If you are a nature lover, schedule a picnic on the gardens, is a really nice experience. Once you could find literally a Crystal Palace there and that's why we still call it Crystal Palace Gardens nowadays. In fact, if you are looking for a beautiful splendid house, forget the idea, nowadays the palace is a sports pavilion that receive some events on the city. So, it is a place worth it for the gardens and to have a nice refreshing walk.

12. PARQUE DA CIDADE

Not in the center of the city you will find another green lungs of the city: Parque da Cidade and the gardens in Serralves. These are two bigger parks that you can go for nice walks or even to run if you are a fan of jogging and wake up before the rest of the family.

Parque da Cidade is the best place in the city to have a walk, spend the afternoon with the family, make a good birthday party for your kid. All the things you can imagine on the lung of the city.

13. JARDINS DE SERRALVES

After visit the Museum you should go to gardens and take a walk and embrace the nature after you had embrace a little bit of culture.

14. SEASIDE (FOZ E MATOSINHOS)

The best think you should do is go from Sé and river side and walk always near the water until you see the differences between the river and the seaside and going from an old part of the city (Foz) with great mansions and also poor neighborhoods and until you arrive at Matosinhos, another city that is known essentially because of the beach and more modern buildings. But please consider that this suggestion is a little harder to do, if you don't like to exercise a lot, use transportation as a car, bus or even a bike.

During the way you will pass through Alfândega do Porto an majestic building that receives also important expositions once in a while and also further you will find a beautiful Lighthouse that is some kind of branding image to the old part of the seaside (Foz).

It is funny to know that this way walking like I say is really hard but there's a tradition on São João night is to do these walking and end in the beach sleeping until sunrise, making fires to feel warmer. This was more traditional few years ago than it is now, maybe because it is difficult to walk such distance on a party night!

15. RIVER

Douro river is a monument and a place to go itself. If you have time, try to make on boat trip that crosses all the bridges that it is totally worth it. Once you are on the river you can have the magical view to the city and to his traditional image of the colorful houses creating some kind of hill.

16. RIVERSIDE

Riverside is the most traditional and authentic part of the city. You need to cross the Sé neighborhood full of authentic Porto spirit and traditions. Just go over the streets until you reach the riverside with a stunning view. Go to the riverside to have dinner, drink a glass of wine, a coffee, or just to enjoy the view and embrace the city.

17. "MIRADOUROS"

Here I could present to you three places that you need to go in order to have a great view to different parts of the city. First, the one that you will be warned about is Passeio das Virtudes – nowadays everyone goes there and just stays drinking beer and watching the sunset on the river. The other is Miradouro São Bento da Vitória – this one is still a kind of secret spot – there's nothing there, only a great view, is not so far from Virtudes in fact, you can go walking from one to another. The other one is not exactly a sightseeing place but once in Porto you should go to Guindalense – a typical Portuguese coffee situated on Escadas dos Guindais and with a great view to the bridge Dom Luis.

18. CULTURE (BOMBARDA)

Before we talk about Bombarda itself, let's talk about the importance of culture in the city of Porto. First things first, the firs projection of our city as a cultural spot was in 2001 with the election of Porto as European Capital of Culture 2001, sharing the title and the focus of the culture this year with Rotterdam. This initiative was accompanied by a strong investment in the recovery and construction of the city's public space. Of note is the restoration of the Garden of Cordoaria of Praça da Batalha and of D. João I Square , and the new buildings, Edifício Transparente (nowadays is deactivated) and Casa da Música.

Now let's talk about the current most important cultural spot in the city (besides Serralves and Casa da Música as well)

With the explosion of tourists and foreigners living on the city, it affects quickly the state of the art, if we can say that. The city started to grow so exponentially that a lot of places were created to share culture and art in his most different ways (photograph, sculpture, painting, performance). Miguel Bombarda was a place almost empty and where no one went before because there was nothing to see there. Nowadays is a street full of Galeries, Art and expositions! If you are a fan of these kinds of things, don't forget to pass there and check what the artist are doing and sharing in the city. You will love.

19. CULTURE (SERRALVES)

Also, you need to go Serralves, but there you need to go even if you are not such an art fan. You can go because of the gardens, you can go because of the mansion or you can because of the expositions center – but definitely you need to go! During the year there's two weekends of party and when everyone go to Serralves and it is really great to see the locals in contact with art in so many ways: the most important is the 48h festival when, as the name say, there's non stop culture theater, performances, concerts, poetry, all the things you can imagine – these use to be on the last weekend of may. Also, in October there's something similar to that but in a smallest portion that is called Festa do Outono and it is a weekend for families to celebrate the beginning of the Autumn season. Check Serralves website to know if you are planning to come in some of these dates.

20. EXPOSITIONS

In Porto you have really nice places with consecrated expositions. On top on of them you have Serralves, then you also have Mercado Ferreira Borges with expositions that come from other cities and stay in exposition most of the times for a few months. Also, you have small places like Centro Português de Fotografia (only about photography) and also the small galleries in Bombarda Street.

21. MONUMENTS AROUND THE CITY

Around the city you will find beautiful monuments and is good for you to recognize some of them:

First, the University Rectory in Cordoaria – is the administrative center of the University and you can enter just to check how beautiful is the building.

It is a rectangular building of neoclassical style , initially destined to the Royal Academy of Navy and Commerce . The initial project is written by Carlos Amarante and dates back to 1807 . During the period of the French invasions and the liberal wars the building works would advance very slowly. The unfinished construction served as a hospital during the siege of Porto (1832-33). In 1833 the project was remodeled by JC Vitória Vila-Nova. The works continued and the initial project still underwent two major renovations, in 1862 , by Gustavo Gonçalves e Sousa, and in 1898, by António Araújo e Silva.

In the building were the Polytechnic Academy of Porto , the College of Orphans, the Academy of Fine Arts, the National Lyceum, the Industrial Institute (predecessor of ISEP until 1933), the Faculty of Engineering (now Faculty of Engineering , until 1937), the Faculty of Economics (until 1974) and the Faculty of Sciences of the University of Porto (until 2007).

At present, the Rectory of the University of Porto

Second, the City Hall, with two wide ramps on either side of the main entrance, access to this modern neoclassical structure is easy (as long as you discount the hill leading to the doors), there is a large clock centred in the building's 70-meter tower, keeping time over the avenida in a most regal way. One of Porto's most famous architects, Correia da Silva, designed the Câmara Municipal and its construction got underway in 1920.

Third, the theaters: Coliseum, Rivoli and Teatro Nacional de São João. Fun facts about these spots: on September 1996 at Coliseum, after a fashion show with Claudia Schiffer , a fire of undetermined origin, completely destroys the box of the stage and causing serious damage in the main room and dressing rooms. The Porto Coliseum reopened on 12 December with the traditional show of the Circo de Natal (that until nowadays is a tradition of christmas time in the city, for all the families on the city). The complete recovery of the room would only be completed two years later reopening to the public on November 24, 1998 , with the opera Carmen in Bizet. As you can see is a open minded cultural spot with different shows and focus. Not only for music and theater. About Rivoli: in the 1970s , the image of the Theater suffered a setback, caused by a bad financial situation. The Rivoli began to deteriorate, with equipment obsolete, without regular programming or own public. In1989, the City Council of Porto decided to buy the structure, in order to return it to the city and its inhabitants. TNSJ - National Theater São João,opened with the comedy "The Vivandeira" the 13 of May of 1798 , in order to mark the birthday of Prince John (John VI), this reason why in the early days, still gave him the name of Teatro do Príncipe .

Other buildings that you will pass by and might want to enter as the Mercado Ferreira Borges (nowadays is the Hard Club – another concert room in the city) and Palácio da Bolsa that you can visit and is a magnificent place full of history.

22. CHURCHES AND CEMETERIES

Like any other city with a lot of history, Porto has monuments that you have to go once you come in the city, at least the most remarkable ones. First, Torre dos Clérigos (and the Church as well), go there and go up to have a great view from the city, then you need to go to other churches that are really beautiful: Igreja de São Francisco - a gothic church in the city of Porto , located in the parish of São Nicolau in the heart of the historical center of Porto, the Construction began in the 14th century as part of a Franciscan convent. Sé Cathedral - the beginning of its construction dates from the first half of the twelfth century , and continued until the beginning of the thirteenth century; Igreja de Santa Clara - built next to the most visible section of the Fernandine Walls, was completed in 1457, as well as the monastery with which it was set, the construction was due to a request from the Poor Clare Franciscan nuns who wanted to replace the very large thirteenth-century monastery; Igreja da Lapa - the cult of Our Lady of Lapa is spread throughout Portugal , Brazil and other former Portuguese colonies, and there are numerous churches dedicated to Nossa Senhora da Lapa and at least, Igreja das Carmelitas - the façade of granite stone work has three entrances with perfect arches , surmounted by an equal number of niches , with the images of Saint Joseph , Saint Teresa of Jesus and Nossa Senhora do Carmo in the center, The upper body contains three windows , the central one being rectangular in shape and the two sides in the shape of a rectangular trapezoid, to finish off the facade a triangular pediment surmounted by balusters, it has a bell tower on the left side, covered in blue monochrome tiles, topped by a bulbous dome.

23. CEMETERIES

May seem strange, but cemeteries in Porto are also great places to feel the history and the beauty of the city, if it is not strange to you, go at least to Agramonte Cemetery (in Boavista).

It is a beautiful place with a lot of Mausoleums with important people in the history of the city and country.

24. ARCHITECTURE

Porto is also connected with architecture. First, because of the Architecture Faculty of the University of Porto that is recognized as one of the best in that area. Also, the city has recognized architects that already won important prizes on the field: Siza Vieira and Eduardo Souto de Moura. Nowadays the city has important buildings representing the contemporary architecture: Casa da Música (Boavista); Vodafone Headquarters (Avenida da Boavista), Serralves Contemporary art museum; Bolhão Subway Station; The Porto Cruise Terminal (South Terminal at

Matosinhos); Architecture House (Matosinhos); and
the Tea House (Leça da Palmeira).

25. PEOPLE

Maybe I am a suspicious person to say this, but I
can bet that you will agree with me: Porto citizens are
the best in the world. They laugh hard, they talk
without any constraint, and even if they don't know
how to speak in English they will help you until last
consequences, without giving up. They will talk to
you about their lives, they will be really nice and even
without talk, and they have a welcome smile that you
don't see a lot of times nowadays. Embrace it and you
will just love that.

26. AIRPORT

The city has one airport: Francisco Sá Carneiro. It
was rebuilt a few years ago and is completely
prepared to welcome you. Once you arrive you can
reach the city center by metro – around 40min trip or
you can take a cab or go by express bus.

27. HOTELS – THE BEST ONES TO STAY

Porto has a lot of renovated hotels that are really nice places to stay if you are kind of fan of some luxury: look for the five stars ones and enjoy the really concept of holiday.

The best rated ones and most luxury as well are: The Yeatman, InterContinental Porto, Flores village Hotel & Spa.

28. HOSTELS – THE BEST ONES TO STAY

Porto has a lot of great hostels that won already a lot of prizes. If you want to stay in a hostel, try to choose the ones like: Rivoli Cinema Hostel (the first hostel in Portugal with a thematic: Cinema – it is really in the center of the city and is a great place to stay); Tattva Design Hostel; Gallery Hostel Porto (in Bombarda), Porto Spot Hostel and Yes Porto Hostel. Check on the Internet and choose the right one for you, they are all really recent and in good conditions, check for the reviews.

29. TRANSPORTS

Metro in Porto is really new (inaugurated in 2002), comparing to other cities at least in Europe. One thing that may confuse you is that you will find a lot of stations over the ground and not underground so it might seem like a tram sometimes, but it is not. The metro connects Porto to the cities where most part of the people lives (Vila Nova de Gaia, Matosinhos, Gaia, Rio Tinto).

On the city you have also a great bus company and in fact you can make a lot of the city only walking because it is not so big.

30. WEATHER

It depends on the place where you come from but most part of the times you will think that the weather in Porto is great. Also, nowadays is kind of hard to predict weather because is really spontaneous sometimes. But, according to the "rules" you will deal with rainy days in months like February and March and the coldest months usually are January and February. Between May and October you will have warm days, big days as well – on the summer the sun sets around 9pm, what is really great. The temperatures rarely go below the 2°, 3° Celsius and above the 30° Celsius.

31. NIGHTLIFE

You need to spend at least one night going out in the city because the nightlife is kind of a highlight for tourists in Porto. Until the beginning of the years 2000 Porto was a totally different city, during the day and mainly during the night. Back in those times the Nightlife was spotted on the riverside but nowadays the night is in the city center and changed a little bit. Now and then one thing remains the same: there's an important influence of the academic life and traditions oh the nightlife in Porto specially in the center.

32. GALERIAS PARIS

Galerias is also the name of the movida in Porto, the citizens say a lot of times "let's go to Galerias" without saying a specifically club or place. Portuguese people like to go out really late at night; you will only see the real movida after 12pm (mainly on Friday and Saturday).

Drink beer on these streets (cheaper and it's not forbidden by law) and late night (around 2pm) go to the clubs like Plano B or Tendinha dos Clérigos and just go out of there with sun again on the streets. Seems hard, but it is a good life that you will enjoy.

Plano B is in fact the most famous club right now. Has always a good list of djs going there on thursdays, friday and saturdays.

Also, go to Piolho Café is a place with an huge academic tradition and you will notice that (if you go between September and June). There you can go eat and stay inside or you can just ask for a beer and stay drinking on the outside. A lot of people do this.

People in Porto and in Portugal (generally) like to go out at night. Not even when you are studying, but even when you are on your thirties, already working. The clubs have this diversification, you will notice.

You have more quiet bares just to get a drink, and the other ones with music and people dancing. They don't differ so much in size, all the clubs are really small, but you will check in the environment.

33. CLUBS

If you are a really a night club fan, you should go to Industria Club that has been renovated and nowadays is a great club to go, on the river side if you feel like a party animal and you don't want to stay only in one zone and you want dance music and great Djs.

Also, in Matosinhos, not in the city center, are localized all the bigger clubs to dance until the sun comes up. Usually, these clubs are frequented by the students and youngest people and typically are the ones where the universities make the bigger parties and events. But if you feel empathy with this spirit, you should go there.

34. MUSIC AND FESTIVALS

During the year Porto receives good concerts at Casa da Música and Coliseum (mostly) but you should be aware that since 2012 the city receives Primavera Sound Festival and it's been a huge success and if you are a festival fan, you need to book your trip considering this! It also helps the city to become more recognized on the last few years and a lot of people came to Porto just because of the festival but then they get in love and they always come back or at least they pretend to!

35. PARTIES YOU DON'T WANT TO MISS

As I said before, the most important party in the city is the night when no one get sleep: from 23th to 24th of June everyone stay on the street and the only objective is to go home with the sun already rise. The most funny thing about these party is not only the fact that the citizens are together celebrating independent on the age, the part that you will not understand (and I don't know if I can in fact explain) is that everyone will be using a plastic hammer – don't hurt, don't get stuck on the hammer part – and the tradition is that you knock everyone's head like saying hello. The other part, that it is a beautiful one – you will see people setting hot air balloons (small ones, not the ones with people inside – don't go so far on your imagination!) and just watching them going through the sky and also check all the lights like stars it gave us some kind of protections and warm feeling. Not so innovative, but also beautiful, you have at midnight a really beautiful firework show on the bridge Dom Luís – if you get a good spot to see it – what is really difficult because as I said everyone is on the street –

you will be speechless and you will never forget this moment.

36. COFFEES – TRADITIONAL ONES TO THE TRENDIEST

On the city you have to discover this old traditional coffees that are really beautiful. First, you need to go to Majestic (in Santa Catarina street). Then you also need to go the old Imperio in Avenida da Liberdade that nowadays is a MacDonald's but keeps the structure of the old coffee and is known as one of the most beautiful McDonald's in the world. Other coffees you can go are: Progresso, Brasileira (that is different nowadays on the inside) and also the one I already told you about: Piolho.

These are the traditional ones, but also you need to know the new ones, mostly on the center of the city, in Galerias Paris and near. Those are trendiest places, where you can to have a coffee or spend the afternoon working on your computer or studying.

37. FOOD

The first thing you will think about and that is mandatory to eat in Porto is Francesinha, the greatest sandwich in the world that is famous for the sauce that is a secret and make all the difference in this typical dish. You can find it in a lot of places but every tourist that arrives in the city use to ask "where can I eat the best francesinha?" and there's no right answer for this in fact, try to look online to reviews and everything and choose the spot you think is the best. Anyway, will be a great experience for you!

Also, we have typical dishes like Cozido à Portuguesa, all the dishes with Bacalhau and Tripas à Moda do Porto.

If food is a core thing to you on a city and while traveling, try to do some kind of typical restaurant route. Go to mandatory places like Casa Guedes, Badalhoca, Casa Portista, Taberna Santo António, Snack-Bar Gazela all of them have typical dishes and are the most traditional in the city.

38. WINE

Maybe the first time you heard someone talking about Porto was related with the wine. In fact, there's an indubitably connection between the city and is wine even if nowadays the tourism is not so focused with that for the youngest at least. But suppositions aside, you need to go to the Porto wine Caves (on Vila Nova de Gaia) and also you need to go there because is an excellent reason to cross the bridge walking and to get to the other side (the river banks are narrow, so it is not a long walk). I am not such an expert in order to recommend the best cave to go, all of them have the same traditions – you visit and then you taste the wine and you have all the explanation of the history that put our city recognized around the world.

39. PORTO WINE CELLARS

The caves are the spaces where the wine ages and its shipped for around the world. On the wine cellars (the most famous ones are Caves Ferreira, Espaço Porto Cruz and Caves Calém – all in Vila Nova de

Gaia) you can have a guided tour to learn all the secrets of the wine and his production and also, in the end, you will have the possibility to taste it.

40. BEER

We were famous because of the wine but nowadays we are becoming more pros on the beer! Super Bock is the brand you will see everywhere – is the most important in the north of the country, if you go south you will see more Sagres and don't get weird if you see a south person discussing with a north one just to discover if Sagres is better than Super Bock, I will not share my opinion but just guess where I came from!

You can drink on the street and at night you will see always a lot of people on the city center just standing, talking and drinking beer on the street and these may seem strange to you but for us is the best plan to weekend nights summer or winter ones.

Nowadays, there's a lot of breweries in the city as well where you can taste really good craft beer – if you are a fan of that just search quickly on the internet and you will find a few.

41. SHOPPING AREA (SANTA CATARINA AND MERCADO DO BOLHÃO)

Santa Catarina is a commercial street with stores that you already know. You should go there because it is a traditional street and with a lot of people walking, most of the times just to check what's new on the fashion stores and enjoying the weekend afternoon. Once there, please go to Mercado Bolhão, a traditional market that has been rebuilded and now has the old place and also a new one that is working only during the rebuilding of the old one.

42. VIA CATARINA SHOPPING MALL

Once in Santa Catarina Street you can go to Via Catarina Shopping Mall. You will find there the traditional stores like Zara, H&M, Fnac, Benetton.

You can find there a lot of places to eat and good stores to buy some clothes or presents to offer.

43. MARKETS

You have some traditional markets but they are being renovated and changing. In Boavista, the old market is now a place with a lot of restaurants and where you can go to taste some good and typical things and you have a lot of choices. Bolhão is the most traditional one and nowadays is being renovated as well. Then, on the other cities you can find the markets that are now new and have a lot of offers on vegetables, fruit and fish: Foz, Matosinhos and Vila Nova de Gaia, you might will pass near them, if you like traditional markets, don't miss the chance to visit them.

44. UNIVERSITY OF PORTO

University of Porto building is located on Praça dos Leões (Cordoaria City Center). It is a central an important building and represent the importance of the University in the city.

University of Porto has a lot of degrees recognized and Medicine, Architecture and Engineering Universities are recognized as the best in the country and occupy and not only in our country, are recognized outside.

Is an important public institution. In fact, in 2017, the University of Porto was among the 300 best universities in the world in QS World University Rankings, international ranking of higher education, being the best place obtained by a higher education and research institution in Portugal.

Also, we received every here more and more erasmus students that have also a great impact in the city dynamic.

45. ACADEMIC TRADITIONS

May seem strange for you to see this topic in a touristic guide, but as a local I am sure that this will be important on your trip. If you visit Porto in months like September, February and May you will notice the academic traditions a lot. University has a lot of rituals in Portugal, specially in Coimbra and in Porto, related to that, you will see a lot of students using the Traje the black academic clothes with a black cape that supposedly was J K Rowling's inspiration to the magic clothes in Harry Potter. In the first week of

May all the students stop everything and just go celebrate the beginning or the end of their degrees – there is a Parade in the city center (if you catch that you will love to see) and also every night there's party in a place near the beach where each university has a spot and a representation and all the students go to the street representing their courses. Also, you will see a lot of young people always with hoodies or t-shirts representing their university.

46. ERASMUS PROGRAM

Maybe seem strange to you to see these here but is important for you to know that University of Porto is a great Academy and it is really recognized worldwide. So, we cannot say that only Ryanair changed the city, Erasmus Program changed it as well. A lot of Erasmus students choose Porto nowadays and they left so in love with the city and the country that they spread it and came back and bring friends and family. The relation between the University and the Principle is also really close which helps these students integration and welcoming.

47. WORK IN PORTO

Ok, you are thinking about holidays and I am talking about work but it's not so illogical. As I already say before, Porto changed a lot in the last years and nowadays is an important creative hub for tech and startups companies. On the city you can find great coworking spaces. A lot of people choose Porto to live and work remotely, so you can "smell" this spirit in a lot of places and that changed the city a little bit as well.

In a few years a lot of Portuguese fresh graduated had to leave the country in order to have better opportunities but nowadays the economy is getting better and they are now returning and bringing new ideas and concepts to our country. Nowadays a lot of startups are installed not only in Lisbon - that is famous as a creative hub spot in all europe - but also is really important in Porto and Braga as well.

Also, a lot of foreigners visit Portugal and then just want to live here and this has a direct impact in the business as well. Also, the erasmus students that come to city to do internships and decide to stay living a few years in the country.

48. FUTEBOL CLUBE DO PORTO

Football is an important thing in Portugal and so it is in the city. On 2004 two major stadiums were built in order to receive the European Football Championship: Estádio do Dragão and Boavista Stadium. Nowadays these are the stadiums of the two biggest football clubs in the city and at least one of them you might have known: Futebol Clube do Porto.

If you are a sports fan you can go visit the stadium or even watch a match. The most important ones are obviously against another european football clubs or with Benfica and Sporting (the other two big clubs from Lisbon).

Football makes the traditional fight between the north and the south of the country, and is the representation of it in fact. It is normal that you heard things like: "the best thing of Lisbon is the highway signal that says Porto".

49. VILA NOVA DE GAIA

Vila Nova de Gaia is another city near Porto. Usually, people say as a joke that the best thing in Vila Nova de Gaia is the view to Porto.

Gaia has and always had a very strong connection to the neighboring city of Porto , not only by sharing the common heritage of Port Wine , but also by the fact that, in the past, the bourgeois and noble families of Porto had, in Vila Nova de Gaia , villas and apartments. In the last decades, due to the economic growth and the improvement of communications with the north bank of the river Douro , Vila Nova de Gaia has gradually received a population that works daily in Porto (mainly due to the construction of the Porto Metro , which stimulated and made these commuting movements between Gaia and Porto even more functional).

You can go walking, just cross the bridge (that is totally worth it), or you can go by transports (like Metro) if you prefer. One possibility is that you cross the bridge top tray and stay a little bit just enjoying the view on Jardim do Morro. Then you can walk until the riverside (where you have the Porto Wine

Caves). Also, you can use the cable car that exists a few years ago and enjoy the view in a different way.

50. MATOSINHOS

Matosinhos is also another city near Porto. It is the best place to go if you like summer, beaches and sun.

On the coast of the city is the port of Leixões , the second largest artificial port of Portugal and second port of the Porto Metropolitan Area . Part of the international airport of Porto covers the municipal boundaries.

Matosinhos was until recently a heavily industrialized municipality, which has become a municipality dedicated to the tertiary sector. However, it still holds oil heritage from the industrial boom. Its main industries are petrochemicals, food and canning, textiles and electrical equipment. It is still a city with a great fishing activity.

It is also in this city, more specifically in the parish of Leça da Palmeira, which is located Exponor , the largest fairground of business in the country. It possessed the most important ports of the Great

Harbor: the Port of Leixões , the largest artificial port of Portugal, built in the late nineteenth century.

TOP REASONS TO BOOK THIS TRIP

Porto is not a big city so is the greatest destination to your next 3 days trip;

It is not an expensive city and it is really trendy nowadays;

Porto citizens are so authentic that will make you feel at home

.

BONUS BOOK

50 THINGS TO KNOW ABOUT PACKING LIGHT FOR TRAVEL

PACK THE RIGHT WAY EVERY TIME

AUTHOR: MANIDIPA BHATTACHARYYA

Edited by Melanie Howthorne

ABOUT THE AUTHOR

Manidipa Bhattacharyya is a creative writer and editor, with an
education in English literature and Linguistics. After working in the IT
industry for seven long years she decided to call it quits and follow her
heart instead. Manidipa has been ghost writing, editing, proof reading
and doing secondary research services for many story tellers and article
writers for about three years. She stays in Kolkata, India with her
husband and a busy two year old. In her own time Manidipa enjoys
travelling, photography and writing flash fiction.

Manidipa believes in travelling light and never carries anything that she
couldn't haul herself on a trip. However, travelling with her child
changed the scenario. She seemed to carry the entire world with her for
the baby on the first two trips. But good sense prevailed and she is
again working her way to becoming a light traveler, this time with a
kid.

INTRODUCTION

*He who would travel happily
must travel light.*

-Antoine de Saint-Exupéry

Travel takes you to different places from seas and mountains to deserts and much more. In your travels you get to interact with different people and their cultures. You will, however, enjoy the sights and interact positively with these new people even more, if you are travelling light.

When you travel light your mind can be free from worry about your belongings. You do not have to spend precious vacation time waiting for your luggage to arrive after a long flight. There is be no chance of your bags going missing and the best part is that you need not pay a fee for checked baggage.

People who have mastered this art of packing light will root for you to take only one carry-on, wherever you go. However, many people can find it really hard to pack light. More so if you are travelling with children. Differentiating between "must have" and "just in case" items is the starting point. There will be ample shopping avenues at your destination which are just waiting to be explored.

69

This book will show you 'packing' in a new 'light' –
pun intended – and help you to embrace light
packing practices for all of your future travels.

Off to packing!

DEDICATION

I dedicate this book to all the travel buffs that I know,
who have given me great insights into the contents of
their backpacks.

THE RIGHT TRAVEL GEAR

1. CHOOSE YOUR TRAVEL GEAR CAREFULLY

While selecting your travel gear, pick items that are
light weight, durable and most importantly, easy to
carry. There are cases with wheels so you can drag
them along – these are usually on the heavy side
because of the trolley. Alternatively a backpack that
you can carry comfortably on your back, or even a
duffel bag that you can carry easily by hand or sling
across your body are also great options. Whatever
you choose, one thing to keep in mind is that the
luggage itself should not weigh a ton, this will give
you the flexibility to bring along one extra pair of
shoes if you so desire.

2. CARRY THE MINIMUM NUMBER OF BAGS

Selecting light weight luggage is not everything. You need to restrict the number of bags you carry as well. One carry-on size bag is ideal for light travel. Most carriers allow one cabin baggage plus one purse, handbag or camera bag as long as it slides under the seat in front. So technically, you can carry two items of luggage without checking them in.

3. PACK ONE EXTRA BAG

Always pack one extra empty bag along with your essential items. This could be a very light weight duffel bag or even a sturdy tote bag which takes up minimal space. In the event that you end up buying a lot of souvenirs, you already have a handy bag to stuff all that into and do not have to spend time hunting for an appropriate bag.

I'm very strict with my packing and have everything in its right place. I never change a rule. I hardly use anything in the hotel room. I wheel my own wardrobe in and that's it.

Charlie Watts

CLOTHES & ACCESSORIES

4. PLAN AHEAD

Figure out in advance what you plan to do on your trip. That will help you to pick that one dress you need for the occasion. If you are going to attend a wedding then you have to carry formal wear. If not, you can ditch the gown for something lighter that will be comfortable during long walks or on the beach.

5. WEAR THAT JACKET

Remember that wearing items will not add extra luggage for your air travel. So wear that bulky jacket that you plan to carry for your trip. This saves space and can also help keep you warm during the chilly flight.

6. MIX AND MATCH

Carry clothes that can be interchangeably used to reinvent your look. Find one top that goes well with a couple of pairs of pants or skirts. Use tops, shirts and jackets wisely along with other accessories like a scarf or a stole to create a new look.

7. CHOOSE YOUR FABRIC WISELY

Stuffing clothes in cramped bags definitely takes its toll which results in wrinkles. It is best to carry wrinkle free, synthetic clothes or merino tops. This will eliminate the need for that small iron you usually bring along.

8. DITCH CLOTHES PACK UNDERWEAR

Pack more underwear and socks. These are the things that will give you a fresh feel even if you do not get a chance to wear fresh clothes. Moreover these are easy to wash and can be dried inside the hotel room itself.

9. CHOOSE DARK OVER LIGHT

While picking your clothes choose dark coloured ones. They are easy to colour coordinate and can last longer before needing a wash. Accidental food spills and dirt from the road are less visible on darker clothes.

10. WEAR YOUR JEANS

Take only one pair of Jeans with you, which you should wear on the flight. Remember to pick a pair that can be worn for sightseeing trips and is equally eloquent for dinner. You can add variety by adding light weight cargoes and chinos.

11. CARRY SMART ACCESSORIES

The right accessory can give you a fresh look even with the same old dress. An intelligent neck-piece, a couple of bright scarves, stoles or a sarong can be used in a number of ways to add variety to your clothing. These light weight beauties can double up as a nursing cover, a light blanket, beach wear, a modesty cover for visiting places of worship, and also makes for an enthralling game of peek-a-boo.

12. LEARN TO FOLD YOUR GARMENTS

Seasoned travellers all swear by rolling their clothes for compact and wrinkle free packing. Bundle packing, where you roll the clothes around a central object as if tying it up, is also a popular method of compact and wrinkle free packing. Stacking folded clothes one on top of another is a big no-no as it makes creases extreme and they are difficult to get rid of without ironing.

13. WASH YOUR DIRTY LAUNDRY

One of the ways to avoid carrying loads of clothes is to wash the clothes you carry. At some places you might get to use the laundry services or a Laundromat but if you are in a pinch, best solution is to wash them yourself. If that is the plan then carrying quick drying clothes is highly recommended, which most often also happen to be the wrinkle free variety.

14. LEAVE THOSE TOWELS BEHIND

Regular towels take up a lot of space, are heavy and take ages to dry out. If you are staying at hotels they will provide you with towels anyway. If you are travelling to a remote place, where the availability of towels look doubtful, carry a light weight travel towel of viscose material to do the job.

15. USE A COMPRESSION BAG

Compression bags are getting lots of recommendation now days from regular travellers. These are useful for saving space in your luggage when you have to pack bulky dresses. While packing for the return trip, get help from the hotel staff to arrange a vacuum cleaner.

FOOTWEAR

16. PUT ON YOUR HIKING BOOTS

If you have plans to go hiking or trekking during your trip, you will need those bulky hiking boots. The best way to carry them is to wear them on flight to save space and luggage weight. You can remove the boots once inside and be comfortable in your socks.

17. PICKING THE RIGHT SHOES

Shoes are often the bulkiest items, along with being the dainty if you are a female. They need care and take up a lot of space in your luggage. It is advisable therefore to pick shoes very carefully. If you plan to do a lot of walking and site seeing, then wearing a pair of comfortable walking shoes are a must. For more formal occasions you can carry durable, light weight flats which will not take up much space.

18. STUFF SHOES

If you happen to pack a pair of shoes, ensure you utilize their hollow insides. Tuck small items like rolled up socks or belts to save space. They will also be easy to find.

TOILETRIES

19. STASHING TOILETRIES

Carry only absolute necessities. Airline rules dictate that for one carry-on bag, liquids and gels must be in 3.4 ounce (100ml) bottles or less, and must be packed in a one quart zip-lock bag. If you are planning to stay in a hotel, the basic things will be provided for you. It's best is to buy the rest from the local market at your destination.

20. TAKE ALONG TAMPONS

Tampons are a hard to find item in a lot of countries. Figure out how many you need and pack accordingly. For longer stays you can buy them online and have them delivered to where you are staying.

21. GET PAMPERED BEFORE YOU TRAVEL

Some avid travellers suggest getting a pedicure and manicure just the day before travelling. This not only gives you a well kept look, you also save the trouble of packing nail polish. Remember, every little bit of weight reduced adds up.

ELECTRONICS

22. LUGGING ALONG ELECTRONICS

Electronics have a large role to play in our lives today. Most of us cannot imagine our lives away from our phones, laptops or tablets. However while travelling, one must consider the amount of weight these electronics add to our luggage. Thankfully smart phones come along with all the essentials tools like a camera, email access, picture editing tools and more. They are smart to the point of eliminating the need to carry multiple gadgets. Choose a smart phone that suits all your requirements and travel with the world in your palms or pocket.

23. REDUCE THE NUMBER OF CHARGERS

If you do travel with multiple electronic devices, you will have to bear the additional burden of carrying all their chargers too. Check if a single charger can be used for multiple devices. You might also consider investing in a pocket charger. These small devices support multiple devices while keeping you charged on the go.

24. TRAVEL FRIENDLY APPS

Along with smart phones come numerous apps, which are immensely helpful in our travels. You name it and you have an app for it at hand – take pictures, sharing with friends and family, torch to light dark roads, maps, checking flight/train times, find hotels and many other things. Use these smart alternatives to traditional items like books to eliminate weight and save space.

I get ideas about what's essential
when packing my suitcase.

-Diane von Furstenberg

TRAVELLING WITH KIDS

25. BRING ALONG THE STROLLER

Kids might enjoy walking for a while but they soon tire out and a stroller is the just the right thing for them to rest in while you continue your tour. Strollers also double duty as a luggage carrier and shopping bag holder. Remember to pick a light weight, easy to handle brand of stroller. Better yet, find out in advance if you can rent a stroller at your destination.

26. BRING ONLY ENOUGH DIAPERS FOR YOUR TRIP

Diapers take up a lot of space and add to the weight of your luggage. Therefore it is advisable to carry just enough diapers to last through the trip and a few for afterwards, till you buy fresh stock at your destination. Unless of course you are travelling to a really remote area, in which case you have no choice but to carry the load. Otherwise diapers are something you will find pretty easily.

27. TAKE ONLY A COUPLE OF TOYS

Children are easily attracted by new things in their environment. While travelling they will find numerous 'new' objects to scrutinize and play with. Packing just one favorite toy is enough, or if there is no favorite toy leave out all of them in favor of stories or imaginary games.

28. CARRY KID FRIENDLY SNACKS

Create a small snack counter in your bag to store away quick bites for those sudden hunger pangs. Depending on the child's age this could include chocolates, raisins, dry fruits, granola bars or biscuits. Also keep a bottle of water handy for your little one.

These things do not add much weight and can be adjusted in a handbag or knapsack.

29. GAMES TO CARRY

Create some travel specific, imaginary games if you have slightly grown up children, like spot the attractions. Keep a coloring book and colors handy for in-flight or hotel time. Apps on your smart phone can keep the children engaged with cartoons and story books. Older children are often entertained by games available on phones or tablets. This cuts the weight of luggage down while keeping the kids entertained.

30. LET THE KIDS CARRY THEIR LOAD

A good thing is to start early sharing of responsibilities. Let your child pick a bag of his or her choice and pack it themselves. Keep tabs on what they are stuffing in their bags by asking if they will be using that item on the trip. It could start out being just an entertainment bag initially but with growing years they will learn to sort the useful from the superfluous. Children as little as four can maneuver a small trolley suitcase like a pro- their experience in pull along toys credit. If you are worried that you may be pulling it for them, you may want to start with a backpack.

31. DECIDE ON LOCATION FOR CHILDREN TO SLEEP

While on a trip you might not always get a crib at your destination, and carrying one will make life all the more difficult. Instead call ahead to see if there are any cribs or roll out beds for children. You may even put blankets on the floor. Weave them a story about camping and they will gladly sleep without any trouble.

32. GET BABY PRODUCTS DELIVERED AT YOUR DESTINATION

If you are absolutely paranoid about not getting your favourite variety of diaper or brand of baby food, check out online stores like amazon.com for services in your destination city. You can buy things online ahead of your travel and get them delivered to your hotel upon arrival.

33. FEEDING NEEDS OF YOUR INFANTS

If you are travelling with a breastfed infant, you save the trouble of carrying bottles and bottle sanitization kits. For special food, or medications, you may need to call ahead to make sure you have a refrigerator where you are staying.

34. FEEDING NEEDS OF YOUR TODDLER

With the progression from infancy to toddler, their dietary requirements too evolve. You will have to pack some snacks for travelling time. Fresh fruits and vegetables can be purchased at your destination. Most of the cities you travel to in whichever part of the world, will have baby food products and formulas, available at the local drug-store or the supermarket.

35. PICKING CLOTHES FOR YOUR BABY

Contrary to popular belief, babies can do without many changes of clothes. At the most pack 2 outfits per day. Pack mix and match type clothes for your little one as well. Pick things which are comfortable to wear and quick to dry.

36. SELECTING SHOES FOR YOUR BABY

Like outfits, kids can make do with two pairs of comfortable shoes. If you can get some water resistant shoes it will be best. To expedite drying wet shoes, you can stuff newspaper in them then wrap

them with newspaper and leave them to dry
overnight.

37. KEEP ONE CHANGE OF CLOTHES HANDY

Travelling with kids can be tricky. Keep a change of
clothes for the kids and mum handy in your purse or
tote bag. This takes a bit of space in your hand
luggage but comes extremely handy in case there are
any accidents or spills.

38. LEAVE BEHIND BABY ACCESSORIES

Baby accessories like their bed, bath tub, car seat, crib
etc. should be left at home. Many hotels provide a
crib on request, while car seats can be borrowed from
friends or rented. Babies can be given a bath in the
hotel sink or even in the adult bath tub with a little bit
of water. If you bring a few bath toys, they can be
used in the bath, pool, and out of water. They can also
be sanitized easily in the sink.

39. CARRY A SMALL LOAD OF PLASTIC BAGS

With children around there are chances of a number
of soiled clothes and diapers. These plastic bags help
to sort the dirt from the clean inside your big bag.

These are very light weight and come in handy to other carry stuff as well at times.

PACK WITH A PURPOSE

40. PACKING FOR BUSINESS TRIPS

One neutral-colored suit should suffice. It can be paired with different shirts, ties and accessories for different occasions. One pair of black suit pants could be worn with a matching jacket for the office or with a snazzy top for dinner.

41. PACKING FOR A CRUISE

Most cruises have formal dinners, and that formal dress usually takes up a lot of space. However you might find a tuxedo to rent. For women, a short black dress with multiple accessory options will do the trick.

42. PACKING FOR A LONG TRIP OVER DIFFERENT CLIMATES

The secret packing mantra for travel over multiple climates is layering. Layering traps air around your body creating insulation against the cold. The same light t-shirt that is comfortable in a warmer climate can be the innermost layer in a colder climate.

REDUCE SOME MORE WEIGHT

43. LEAVE PRECIOUS THINGS AT HOME

Things that you would hate to lose or get damaged leave them at home. Precious jewelry, expensive gadgets or dresses, could be anything. You will not require these on your trip. Leave them at home and spare the load on your mind.

44. SEND SOUVENIRS BY MAIL

If you have spent all your money on purchasing souvenirs, carrying them back in the same bag that you brought along would be difficult. Either pack everything in another bag and check it in the airport or get everything shipped to your home. Use an international carrier for a secure transit, but this could be more expensive than the checking fees at the airport.

45. AVOID CARRYING BOOKS

Books equal to weight. There are many reading apps which you can download on your smart phone or tab.

Plus there are gadgets like Kindle and Nook that are thinner and lighter alternatives to your regular book.

CHECK, GET, SET, CHECK AGAIN

46. STRATEGIZE BEFORE PACKING

Create a travel list and prepare all that you think you need to carry along. Keep everything on your bed or floor before packing and then think through once again – do I really need that? Any item that meets this question can be avoided. Remove whatever you don't really need and pack the rest.

47. TEST YOUR LUGGAGE

Once you have fully packed for the trip take a test trip with your luggage. Take your bags and go to town for window shopping for an hour. If you enjoy your hour long trip it is good to go, if not, go home and reduce the load some more. Repeat this test till you hit the right weight.

48. ADD A ROLL OF DUCT TAPE

You might wonder why, when this book has been talking about reducing stuff, we're suddenly asking you to pack something totally unusual. This is because when you have limited supplies, duct tape is immensely helpful for small repairs – a broken bag, leaking zip-lock bag, broken sunglasses, you name it and duct tape can fix it, temporarily.

49. LIST OF ESSENTIAL ITEMS

Even though the emphasis is on packing light, there are things which have to be carried for any trip. Here is our list of essentials:

• Passport/Visa or any other ID

• Any other paper work that might be required on a trip like permits, hotel reservation confirmations etc.

• Medicines – all your prescription medicines and emergency kit, especially if you are travelling with children

• Medical or vaccination records

• Money in foreign currency if travelling to a different country

• Tickets- Email or Message them to your phone

50. MAKE THE MOST OF YOUR TRIP

Wherever you are going, whatever you hope to do we encourage you to embrace it whole-heartedly. Take in the scenery, the culture and above all, enjoy your time away from home.

On a long journey even a straw
weighs heavy.

-Spanish Proverb

PACKING AND PLANNING TIPS

A Week before Leaving

- Arrange for someone to take care of pets and water plants.

- Stop mail and newspaper.

- Notify Credit Card companies where you are going.

- Change your thermostat settings.

- Car inspected, oil is changed, and tires have the correct pressure.

- Passports and photo identification is up to date.

- Pay bills.

- Copy important items and download travel Apps.

- Start collecting small bills for tips.

Right Before Leaving

- Clean out refrigerator.

- Empty garbage cans.

- Lock windows.

- Make sure you have the proper identification with you.

- Bring cash for tips.

- Remember travel documents.

- Lock door behind you.

- Remember wallet.

- Unplug items in house and pack chargers.

>TOURIST

READ OTHER
GREATER THAN A TOURIST
BOOKS

Greater Than a Tourist San Miguel de Allende Guanajuato Mexico:
50 Travel Tips from a Local by Tom Peterson

Greater Than a Tourist – Lake George Area New York USA:
50 Travel Tips from a Local by Janine Hirschklau

Greater Than a Tourist – Monterey California United States:
50 Travel Tips from a Local by Katie Begley

Greater Than a Tourist – Chanai Crete Greece:
50 Travel Tips from a Local by Dimitra Papagrigoraki

Greater Than a Tourist – The Garden Route Western Cape Province
South Africa: 50 Travel Tips from a Local by Li-Anne McGregor van
Aardt

Greater Than a Tourist – Sevilla Andalusia Spain:
50 Travel Tips from a Local by Gabi Gazon

Greater Than a Tourist – Kota Bharu Kelantan Malaysia:
50 Travel Tips from a Local by Aditi Shukla

Children's Book: Charlie the Cavalier Travels the World by Lisa
Rusczyk

93

> TOURIST

Visit Greater Than a Tourist for Free Travel Tips
http://GreaterThanATourist.com

Sign up for the Greater Than a Tourist Newsletter for discount days, new books, and travel information:
http://eepurl.com/cxspyf

Follow us on Facebook for tips, images, and ideas:
https://www.facebook.com/GreaterThanATourist

Follow us on Pinterest for travel tips and ideas:
http://pinterest.com/GreaterThanATourist

Follow us on Instagram for beautiful travel images:
http://Instagram.com/GreaterThanATourist

> TOURIST

Please leave your honest review of this book on Amazon and Goodreads. Please send your feedback to GreaterThanaTourist@gmail.com as we continue to improve the series. We appreciate your positive and constructive feedback. Thank you.

METRIC CONVERSIONS

TEMPERATURE

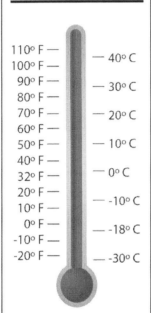

110° F — — 40° C
100° F —
90° F — — 30° C
80° F —
70° F — — 20° C
60° F —
50° F — — 10° C
40° F —
32° F — — 0° C
20° F —
10° F — — -10° C
0° F —
-10° F — — -18° C
-20° F — — -30° C

To convert F to C:

Subtract 32, and then multiply by 5/9 or .5555.

To Convert C to F:

Multiply by 1.8
and then add 32.

32F = 0C

LIQUID VOLUME

To Convert:.................Multiply by
U.S. Gallons to Liters............... 3.8
U.S. Liters to Gallons 26
Imperial Gallons to U.S. Gallons 1.2
Imperial Gallons to Liters....... 4.55
Liters to Imperial Gallons 22
1 Liter = .26 U.S. Gallon
1 U.S. Gallon = 3.8 Liters

DISTANCE

To convert ....Multiply by
Inches to Centimeters 2.54
Centimeters to Inches 39
Feet to Meters....................... .3
Meters to Feet 3.28
Yards to Meters 91
Meters to Yards 1.09
Miles to Kilometers 1.61
Kilometers to Miles............ .62
1 Mile = 1.6 km
1 km = .62 Miles

WEIGHT

1 Ounce = .28 Grams
1 Pound = .4555 Kilograms
1 Gram = .04 Ounce
1 Kilogram = 2.2 Pounds

TRAVEL QUESTIONS

- Do you bring presents home to family or friends after a vacation?

- Do you get motion sick?

- Do you have a favorite billboard?

- Do you know what to do if there is a flat tire?

- Do you like a sun roof open?

- Do you like to eat in the car?

- Do you like to wear sun glasses in the car?

- Do you like toppings on your ice cream?

- Do you use public bathrooms?

- Did you bring your cell phone and does it have power?

- Do you have a form of identification with you?

- Have you ever been pulled over by a cop?

- Have you ever given money to a stranger on a road trip?

- Have you ever taken a road trip with animals?

- Have you ever went on a vacation alone?

- Have you ever run out of gas?

- If you could move to any place in the world, where would it be?

- If you could travel anywhere in the world, where would you travel?

- If you could travel in any vehicle, which one would it be?

- If you had three things to wish for from a magic genie, what would they be?

- If you have a driver's license, how many times did it take you to pass the test?

- What are you the most afraid of on vacation?

- What do you want to get away from the most when you are on vacation?

- What foods smells bad to you?

- What item do you bring on ever trip with you away from home?

- What makes you sleepy?

- What song would you love to hear on the radio when you're cruising on the highway?

- What travel job would you want the least?

- What will you miss most while you are away from home?

- What is something you always wanted to try?

- What is the best road side attraction that you ever saw?

- What is the farthest distance you ever biked?

- What is the farthest distance you ever walked?

- What is the weirdest thing you needed to buy while on vacation?

- What is your favorite candy?

- What is your favorite color car?

- What is your favorite family vacation?

- What is your favorite food?

- What is your favorite gas station drink or food?

- What is your favorite license plate design?

- What is your favorite restaurant?

- What is your favorite smell?

- What is your favorite song?

- What is your favorite sound that nature makes?

- What is your favorite thing to bring home from a vacation?

- What is your favorite vacation with friends?

- What is your favorite way to relax?

- Where is the farthest place you ever traveled in a car?

- Where is the farthest place you ever went North, South, East and West?

- Where is your favorite place in the world?

- Who is your favorite singer?

- Who taught you how to drive?

- Who will you miss the most while you are away?

- Who if the first person you will contact when you get to your destination?

- Who brought you on your first vacation?

- Who likes to travel the most in your life?

- Would you rather be hot or cold?

- Would you rather drive above, below, or at the speed limited?

- Would you rather drive on a highway or a back road?

- Would you rather go on a train or a boat?

- Would you rather go to the beach or the woods?

TRAVEL BUCKET LIST

1.

2.

3.

4.

5.

6.

7.

8.

9.

10.

NOTES

Printed in Great Britain
by Amazon